THE BOURNE SOCIETY

THEN AND NOW

The Changing Scene
of
Surrey Life
in

Caterham, Chaldon, Chipstead, Coulsdon, Godstone, Hooley, Kenley, Purley, Sanderstead, Warlingham, Whyteleafe and Woldingham.

Dedicated to the memory of the late James Batley

The cover photograph c.1904
shows a typical scene outside
Gardner's Tea Rooms, Riddlesdown

First Published 1986
Reprinted 1987
© The Bourne Society 1986
The Bourne Society
17 Manor Avenue,
Caterham, Surrey
CR3 6AP

ISBN O 900992 28 X

Typeset and Printed by Lyndhurst Printing Company Limited
Hardley Industrial Estate, Hythe, Southampton SO4 6ZX

Printed in England

Foreword

The RT. HON. SIR GEOFFREY HOWE, QC. MP.

As a member of the Bourne Society for more than a decade, my knowledge of the local history of many parts of my constituency has been much added to by the work of its enthusiastic members. This fascinating compilation by the members of the Photographic Group will be appreciated not only by all those who know this part of Surrey, but also by a wider audience interested in the changes of English society.

Inevitably the old photographs often look the most attractive: horses and carts seem more interesting than motor cars, the form of dress looks somehow charming, the buildings are more overgrown, the focus seems more gentle. Yet we should beware of the national vice of romanticising the past: modern is often better than old; sometimes the things which look attractive to us now were those least popular with contemporaries; and of course modern high quality camera equipment produces a sharper and harsher image of reality.

Change is inescapable, often desirable. But if we understand our history we are better able to shape change to our own purposes, to secure continuity in our communities, to preserve what is best. This publication is an aid to that understanding in the Bourne Society area.

For the less serious-minded, it is simply a very interesting illustration of "Then and Now"!

HOUSE OF COMMONS

1986

Preface

The Photographic Group of the Bourne Society consists of a small number of keen amateur photographers who share an interest in local history.

The idea for the project came from our members but their enthusiasm was inspired by a similar publication produced by the Send & Ripley History Society, to whom we are most grateful for their help and encouragement. It has been a pleasure to work with such an able and enthusiastic team and we are grateful for the support received from the Council of the Bourne Society and also from members and friends who encouraged us to complete the project.

We are dedicating the book to the memory of the late James Batley, a past member of the Society, who did so much to promote an interest in local history.

Grahame W. Brooks
Photographic Group Leader
The Bourne Society

* * *

Sources

The information in this publication has been obtained from many sources. Anyone wishing to study in more depth should find the following publications of interest;

Godstone Explored - Tandridge District Council
Godstone in 1900 - Godstone Preservation Society
History of Woldingham and Marden Park - John Greenwood - The Bourne Society
Jubilee History Caterham and Warlingham - James Batley - The Bourne Society
Local History Records - The Bourne Society
R.A.F. Kenley - Peter Flint - Terence Dalton
The Caterham Railway - Jeoffry Spence - The Oakwood Press

It is inevitable in producing a publication of this kind that errors and omissions will occur. We apologise for any that may be found and would welcome comments from readers.

Acknowledgements

The task of producing this book was undertaken by the following members of the Photographic Group, each of whom took responsibility for a particular part of the Bourne Society area;

Dorothy Tutt, Ronald Dabbs, Roger Packham, Paul Sandford, Ivon Teear and Grahame Brooks.

Acknowledgement is also due to the many members and friends of the Society who gave help and advice;

Miss. N. Batley
Mr. Maurice Cooke
Mr. John Cooper
Mr. David Garrard
Mr. Roger Gambell
Mr. Geoff Harris

Mr. Len Heal
Mr. Victor Malempre
Mrs. D.N. Neilson
Mrs. Mary Saaler
Mr. Roy Scott
Mr. Peter Skuse

Mr. Len Muggeridge for drawing the map of the Bourne area.

We also wish to thank the following organisations;
Mobil Oil Centenary Fund for a donation to assist the project.
R.A.F. Museum - Hendon for permission to reproduce the photograph of Kenley aerodrome.

Introduction

Through the medium of this book we invite you to join us on a journey through space and time. Because the space includes several places of equal interest the arrangement is alphabetical, and a map is included for reference. Regarding time, the majority of the 'Then' scenes were captured during the Edwardian era, and all have a 'Now' view for comparison.

When the Bourne Society was launched in 1956 the area of study was defined as being the Urban District of Coulsdon and Purley, and the Urban District of Caterham and Warlingham. Local Government reorganisation has brought changes in name and status, but our area of interest remains as before, with the addition of Chipstead and Godstone. The Society has a membership total of around 1350, and members who move away from the area frequently retain their interest. In the thirty years since this Society was founded much work has been done, and by means of our annual publication 'Local History Records' it has been possible to create a permanent record to which we can all refer. (25 volumes to date.)

Why 'The Bourne Society'? A bourne is a stream of irregular flow, and it is a factor common to both of our original Urban Districts. The two principal valleys in our part of north east Surrey are, in geological terms, 'dry', but there is, in fact, quite a considerable underground flow of natural water from rainfall. Quantity varies greatly, but when it builds up beyond the capacity of the natural drainage system the water rises to the surface and appears as a bourne. Near the railway bridge over Marlpit Lane, near Coulsdon South Station, it is possible to hear the water moving through the modern drainage channel, while the other stream, coming along the valley from the direction of Caterham, flows in an open ditch for some distance along its route. At Purley these two streams meet, and the water flow continues towards Croydon, joining other natural springs to form the Wandle and ultimately flowing into the Thames. The modern drainage is usually adequate, but even today there is occasional flooding. From time to time in the past it was very bad, and such floods gave rise to the superstitious belief that it forewarned of a national disaster. Certainly it could be a local disaster for those unfortunate residents whose homes and land were flooded.

The fact that the valleys tended to be wet has influenced our development. Palaeolithic Man was hereabouts some 200 to 300,000 years ago, as witnessed by the Acheulian handaxes found in Chaldon and Coulsdon. Other artefacts and early sites bring us through Middle and New Stone Age, Bronze, Iron Age and Romano-British periods, demonstrating a small but continuous thread of habitation. When our present village settlements were created, they were all established on higher ground.

The feudal lords gave much of the land to the use of the religious foundations, and up to the time of the Dissolution of the Monasteries, abbeys such as Chertsey and Waltham, and priories such as Merton and Tandridge could be numbered amongst those who had an interest here. After them came the local landowners, who built fine houses for themselves and their clergy. Being primarily an agricultural area there were large numbers of farmhouses, but many have been demolished. Probably the oldest building, aside from the churches, is Taunton Manor, whose history can be traced back to the early 13th. century. Chaldon Court dates in part from the 14th. century, but the exteriors of these buildings give the casual passerby little or no clue to such early origins. All buildings undergo change over the centuries, and our parish churches are no exception. Each is different from the next, and all have features worthy of note. Only one or two will be found in these pages, as generally speaking, other scenes provide greater interest.

At first the coming of the railway made only a slight impact as regards increased population, but by the time the 19th. century was drawing to a close Caterham in the Valley, Whyteleafe, Purley and Coulsdon-Smitham Bottom were all established growing communities. The old villages on the hills were only gradually changing, but by 1930 the breaking up of local estates released much land into the hands of the property developer.

There is not space to give a full history of the postcard here, but by soon after 1900 cards were available in Britain depicting local scenes. Collecting these became very popular, and many thousands were sent each year up to the 1914/18 war period. We are greatly indebted to those early photographers who, by virtue of their work or purely through interest and enthusiasm as amateurs, recorded so many of the everyday scenes and current events of that era, now long past.

Dorothy Tutt.

The Bourne Society area showing the origins of the Bourne.

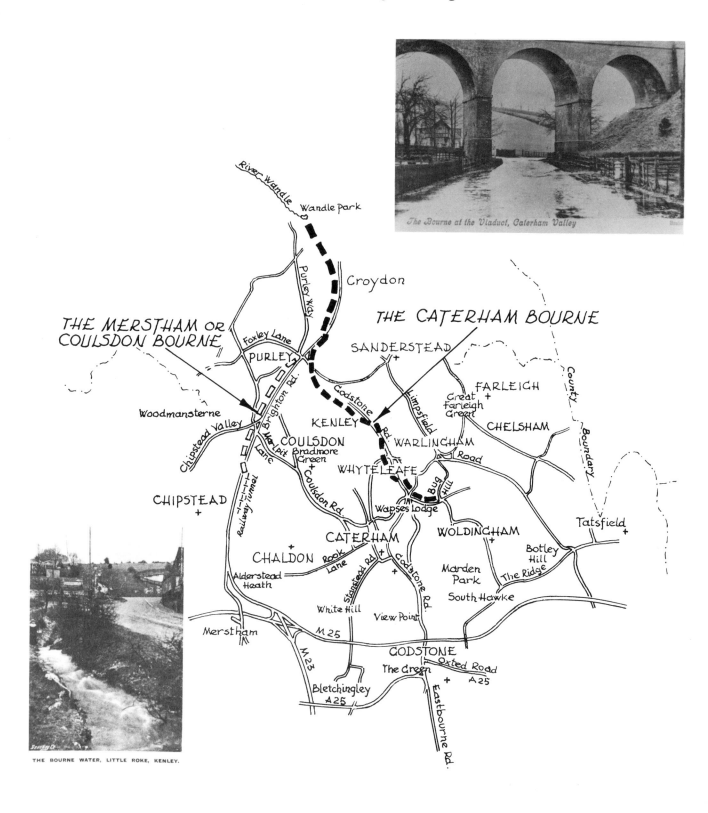

The Bourne at the Viaduct, Caterham Valley

River Wandle

Wandle Park

Croydon

Purley Way

THE MERSTHAM OR COULSDON BOURNE

Foxley Lane

PURLEY

THE CATERHAM BOURNE

SANDERSTEAD

FARLEIGH

Great Farleigh Green

CHELSHAM

County Boundary

Woodmansterne

Brighton Rd.

Chipstead Valley

KENLEY

Godstone Rd.

Limpsfield

COULSDON

Marlpit Lane

Bradmore Green

WARLINGHAM

Road

WHYTELEAFE

Bug Hill

Railway Tunnel

CHIPSTEAD

Coulsdon Rd.

Wapses Lodge

Tatsfield

CATERHAM

WOLDINGHAM

Botley Hill

The Ridge

CHALDON

Rook Lane

Alderstead Heath

Stanstead Rd.

Godstone Rd.

Marden Park

South Hawke

White Hill

View Point

Merstham

M25

M23

GODSTONE

Oxted Road A25

The Green

Bletchingley A25

Eastbourne Rd.

THE BOURNE WATER, LITTLE ROKE, KENLEY.

6

Caterham

The Snailway Train!

CATERHAM

EXPRESS

Couldn't write before—
Have only just arrived

Caterham, in reality comprises two separate communities, Caterham on the Hill and Caterham Valley. Caterham on the Hill which was called Upper Caterham in the early years of this century is the original village. St. Lawrence's Church dates from around 1100 AD, whilst 84 High Street and 5/7 Town End date from the first half of the 17th Century.

Caterham Valley has grown up as a direct result of the construction of the branch railway line from Purley, opened in 1856. Prior to that time the valley was entirely rural. Church Hill now connects the two communities but the much older route, Waller Lane is still used by pedestrians.

HIGH STREET, UPPER CATERHAM.

This view is from the south end of the High Street, Caterham on the Hill, looking towards the village. Beyond the horse and cart is a glimpse of No. 84 which dates from the early 17th century. It has been occupied by the Hills family for many years.

The fine Cedar tree, prominent in the modern view in the centre of the pavement, was, before the road widening in June 1936, in the grounds of the Old Rectory.

8

A 1920s view of the Old Rectory, a small part of which could possibly date from as early as the 16th century. It was last used for its original purpose by the Rev'd Kenneth Budd in 1970. After some years as flats it was in 1984, sold to a local firm of Builders. W.R.Buxton Ltd., and thereby saved from demolition.

The interior has been turned into offices, whilst the exterior has been tastefully repaired and restored. The fine Cedar tree, the branches of which can be seen in the modern photograph, now stands outside the grounds. It has an estimated age of more than 250 years.

In the High Street, north of the Old Rectory stood the thatched Box Cottage, home of the Riches family. Further along at the junction with Park Road was Mr. and Mrs. Brazier's flower and vegetable shop. This corner shop still stands but the flint wall was demolished in the 1930s when the Co-operative Store (at present empty) was built in the garden

Other shops now stand on the site of Box Cottage, but in the distance in both views, the Blacksmiths Arms public house can be seen.

A 1930s view of the High Street, with the Blacksmiths Arms on the right and the King and Queen public house on the left. In the far distance in the old view are the houses in Town End which were demolished in 1973 to make way for further development of the Raglan Precinct flats and shops.

Caterham High Street from the junction with Chaldon Road, around 1905. The ironmonger's shop, left foreground, was owned by Mr. Robert Vigar, Captain of the Fire Brigade and a prominent local citizen at the turn of the century. The Fire Engine, which was horse drawn, was kept in the Fire Engine House, the low building on the right with a turret.

Further along on the right can be seen in both photographs the projecting windows belonging to the upper floor of the old Soldiers Home. This has now been converted into shops and the Raja Tandoori Restaurant.

A view of Chaldon Road in the early 1900s with Vigar's stores in the far distance. The Board School (Hillcroft), built in 1872, is obscured by the trees on the right. On the left, the shops from the near end were Coulings, Corn and Seed Merchant, Daughtreys fruit and vegetable shop; Swarmans, Newsagents and Confectioners; Greenslades, ham and beef stores; Hollicks, Confectioners. Next were three cottages, and lastly Mr. Lock, Plumber.

By 1971 the whole of this row had been demolished to make way for the Raglan Precinct, but the Golden Lion public house remains on the corner site.

13

Caterham, Station Approach.

In the Valley, Caterham Station, terminus of the branch line from Purley, was rebuilt just prior to 1900, when the original single track was doubled. Waitrose Store, built 1982, now stands to the right of the station.

In the distance is Church Hill, leading to Caterham on the Hill. The Railway Hotel, later known until 1982, as the Valley Hotel, is now run by the Pizza Hut Company.

For many years a fountain, surmounted by a gas lamp was the central feature of the Square, and can be seen in this view dated 1910.

Today a roundabout dominates the Square, while the fountain may now be found in White Knobs Recreation Ground.

Croydon Road, Caterham Valley, around 1930. The open space on the far right which was allotments, is now occupied by Woolworths Store.

The upper floors of the buildings have changed little over the years but the shop fronts have altered considerably.

Another view of Croydon Road, Caterham Valley, showing more clearly on the right the open space now occupied by Woolworths Store. The shops on the left in the old photograph were Chapmans, Drapers; E.J. Higgins, Stationers and Booksellers; the Caterham Printing Works which printed the Caterham and Purley Weekly Press; the South Surburban Co-operative Store.

Chaldon

Chaldon is one of the oldest communities in the Bourne area and has preserved a charm of its own. In the turn-of-the-century scene above, Ditches Lane meanders north to Chaldon's Parish Church. On the right - Willey Farm on the Pilgrim's Way at Chaldon.

Chaldon Church.

The Church of St. Peter and St. Paul at Chaldon, one of the oldest churches in the Bourne district, celebrates its novocentenary in 1986. The photographic record shows little change, save the maturing of tree and shrub surrounding the church. This pattern is repeated throughout the nearby residential districts. The once bare downland is now thick with mature trees - many assured longevity through vigilance of citizens and Tree Preservation Orders!

Chipstead

CHIPSTEAD CHURCH, NR. COULSDON.   28.

J.T. Carey
Real Photo Series.

The village of Chipstead, part of the modern borough of Reigate and Banstead, is located in the rural south-west area of the Bourne Society's interest. The ancient parish is centred on a hill, high above the A23 at Hooley and it also has common boundaries with Banstead, Coulsdon, Gatton, Kingswood, Merstham and Woodmansterne.

St. Margaret's is a noble church and Chipstead also has several ancient farms and a collection of interesting houses of differing styles, not least in the hamlet of Mugswell. In the present century, Chipstead has retained much of its rural charm for the benefit of a community so close to the urban sprawl of Greater London.

The old Post Office, or No.1 Shabden Cottages, is pictured in about 1912 and the distinguished looking lady may well be the post mistress referred to by Eric Parker in 'Surrey Highways & Byeways'. The ivy covered house remains largely unaltered and is a private residence; the pillar box has been moved across the road. The building was originally the National School.

In the modern view, the Peter Aubertin Hall may just be seen on the left.

In the charming summer view of Elmore Pond, High Road, taken in about 1913, a brewery van belonging to the Mitcham and Cheam Brewery Company is captured for posterity by an anonymous photographer.

In the spring of 1986. the pond is still backed by some pleasing trees, not yet in leaf and the reflections convey a peaceful scene interrupted only by the increased volume of traffic. The frozen nature of the pond had deceived more than one motorist to park there in the Winter of 1985/6 with disasterous results! Note the rugby posts of Chipstead R.F.C.

Fifty years separate these two photographs of Elmore Pond Cottages and Elmore Pond, looking south-west towards the junction of Castle Hill with High Road.

The cottages have undergone a sympathetic extension in recent years but otherwise the scene has changed but little this century. The scout hut may be seen to the left of the older photograph. The building was originally an eighteenth century farmhouse.

The White Hart, at the junction of Hazelwood Lane and High Road, has been a public house since at least 1775. The old view dates from around 1912 when F. Adams was the licensee and an interesting collection of vehicles is left outside.

The central island remains, treeless, and the advertising posters on the fence in High Road have given way to a toilet block and a car park entrance. Page & Overton's Brewery was situated in Croydon.

chipstead village. 2

These views show Gatefield Cottages in the High Road, looking towards the entrance with Starrock Lane. The cottages were built on part of Gatehouse and Shop fields by Frank Goad of Chipstead Lodge at the turn of the present century and they now back on to the public open space known as The Meads.

The old view was taken in about 1913 and an elegantly dressed lady walks past the cottages on a summer's day reflecting, no doubt, on the luxuriant foliage and the lengthening shadows.

A turn into Starrock Lane from High Road, looking east, shows two very different forms of transport and the views are distanced by some 73 years. The horse-drawn vehicle is probably a baker's delivery van and attracts the attention of the local residents.

The left hand house has gained two modern windows, but has lost its hedges and gate.

On the right of the picture is Vincent's Green and, just out of view, is Palmer's Cottage which dates from the eighteenth century.

The course for Chipstead Golf Club was laid out in 1905 as part of the Stagbury Estate developed by Mrs. Vade Walpole and an Edwardian date is still proudly displayed on the Club House.

The old view was taken prior to the Great War and is remarkable for the panoramic scene which is now obscured by trees.

Much development has taken place in the Chipstead Valley. On the far right of the early photograph may be seen the Chipstead Station building.

Chipstead and Banstead Downs Station is pictured a year or two before the outbreak of the Great War. The level-crossing gates and signal box, removed in 1953 and 1965 respectively, can clearly be seen and there are two trolleys on the up platform, which would not be in evidence today. However, the station retains its former character but note the change in lighting, the replacement fence and the flower border.

Two formally dressed ladies with walking sticks stand where Lackford Road now interrupts the line of shops leading to Chipstead Station. The date is some time prior to July, 1914, and the smooth downlands behind the railway line (part of Chipstead Golf Club) are now concealed by woodland.

Note that the entrance canopy to the station has disappeared and that the little greenhouse in the centre of the old photograph has been replaced by a rather ugly parade of shops.

Coulsdon

The Fox has been a favourite watering-hole for residents of Old Coulsdon and visiting ramblers to Coulsdon Common and Farthing Downs alike. The fine Chestnut tree, where weary hikers rested, has made way for an enlarged car park. The Fox still retains its appeal after a major refurbishment in 1986.

Badmore Green, Coulsdon.   G&E.Leisten.

This Old Coulsdon scene at Bradmore Green has changed little over the years.

The continued efforts of nearby residents have kept the area free of litter and the pond unspoiled by rusting bicycles, bedsteads etc. as befitting a conservation area.

Looking north along the Brighton Road at Smitham Bottom, this scene of about 1905 shows an already busy community which was growing around the railway, the lime works and Cane Hill Asylum. Today the A23 arterial road slices Coulsdon west from east; bypass plans are pending in 1986 to ease congestion. Traders and residents don't always see eye to eye on the best solution for the community!

" Ye Red Lion," Smitham Bottom.

Modified and rebuilt several times in its history, not least since wartime bombing, the Red Lion remains a Coulsdon landmark - in an area not well endowed with pubs! Much of the land released for building in the district has restrictive covenants imposed by their erstwhile Temperance landlords!

The entrance to Cane Hill drive in 1908 with Lion Green Road stretching away to bare, undeveloped downland.

On the corner with the Brighton Road the tea and dining rooms of Coppards's Temperance Hotel (built 1891) provided a favourite halt for cyclists. Today, the traffic hurtles north off the motorways and stopping is barely encouraged!

Cane Hill Asylum.

The ivy has long gone from Cane Hill and now, over a century after it opened its doors to patients in 1883, this institution, so instrumental in the growth of Coulsdon, is due to close. The community awaits the fate of this piece of Green Belt land with concern.

An infants' class of 1906 at Smitham Bottom Council Mixed School at Chipstead Valley Road. With beginnings at Lion Green in 1886, educating the children of staff at the newly opened Cane Hill Asylum, Smitham School has adapted and grown with the community.

In 1986 a centenary of achievement and service to Coulsdon is celebrated by the school. For many years yet another new Smitham School has been mooted. In 1986 plans are to be advanced for a new school off Portnalls Road. Perhaps some part of the old can escape the developers to continue serving the community and providing a link with the past?

Godstone

We're Having a
H"OWL"ING TIME
AT
GODSTONE

The story of Godstone is the 'Tale of Two Villages'. The old village lies around the Church, perhaps once the site of a Saxon Minster. Church Town with its timber-framed houses has a quiet rural atmosphere which is very different from the busy area around Godstone Green. The modern village of Godstone developed during the 16th and 17th centuries and by the 19th century it was a flourishing community with a daily carriage service to London, four inns, a malt house and brewery, a post-office and several tailors and dressmakers as well as many suppliers of foodstuffs. In the 20th century, by-passed by motorways, Godstone provides the visitor with a chance to study its history by quietly contemplating its buildings.

The house on the left is part of the 'Island'. It was once owned by a plumber and the wooden extension was his workshop. To the north is Needlesbank. Beneath some of the houses are the blocked entrances to sand mines. The Victorian house on the right was called 'Cavern House' indicating an entrance to the mines.

Hare and Hounds, Godstone

The building dates from the 16th century; inside was Long Robin's Bar where once an inscription declared 'In 17 hundred and sixty-six Long Robin laid this floor with bricks, Welcome Inn'.
In 1851 the innkeeper was George Steer who was also the parish clerk and surveyor of the roads.

In the field behind the Hare and Hounds is the base of a windmill. It was a post-mill and the hole for the centre post can still be seen in the top of the mound.

Godstone, High Street.

On the right are Clayton's Cottages of 18th century date. The shop projecting on to the street was once a chemist's and the somewhat eccentric proprietor, Mr. Edgar, had eight locks and bolts on the door. It was later acquired by the Brooker family who were the village hairdressers for many years. They ran it as a newsagent's and tobacconists's shop.

The building opposite 'Brookers' was once the village 'lock-up' which later became the Fire Station. The fire engine was horse-drawn and pumped by hand. The Station closed in 1946 and the building was used as the Parish Council Offices.

The Bell Inn is one of the oldest buildings in Godstone, dating from the early 15th century. In the 19th century it was a prosperous coaching inn and had a wide entrance in the front to allow coaches and carriages to pass into the yard.

Opposite the Bell was the Greyhound Inn which was built as an inn in the late 16th century. It later became Garston Farm and is now the Godstone Hotel.

Close to St. Nicholas' Church are St. Mary's Homes (almshouses) built in 1872 to a design by Sir Gilbert Scott. Eight houses and a chapel are set around a court-yard.

The romantic Victorian appearance of these homes blends well with the still rural character of Church Lane.

Ivy Mill, Godstone.

The mill-house of Thomas Northey, apothecary, is described in a document of 1698: For £40, the carpenter, Charles Ridley, agreed to build a house of four rooms with a central chimney, four windows and a tiled porch. The cost also included building a barn and stables. Behind the mill an embankment retained the water for the mill-pond.

The mill in Ivy Mill Lane burned down in the 1920s, and the pond has since been drained.

42

The Old Post Office & General Store, now run by Mr. and Mrs. Sperry, has changed very little. It was formerly the Empire Stores built in 1904 near South Godstone Station. The station had been opened in 1842 on the Redhill to Tonbridge line and soon a small community of railway workers was established around the station.

A traveller in about 1907 describes 'a ridiculous station, put down in the middle of a country road bearing a name to which it had no right whatever …Here I tried the inn near the station - it was a cheerless hole full of tramps. I should not like to spend those three hours at Godstone Station again'!

Hooley

Hooley can claim to be little more than a parade of shops and a row of houses, some Victorian, on either side of the Brighton Road (A 23) between Merstham and Coulsdon. In the earlier years of this century it had a much stronger village identity and even had its own forge. Hooley is overlooked by Netherne Hospital to the east and by Chipstead to the west and until recently its best known feature was The Star public house, pictured above c.1914. This building was originally a farm house and was sacrificed to the motor car a few years ago when the road was straightened.

MOUNT PLEASANT TEA HOUSE, BRIGHTON ROAD, MERSTHAM, SURREY.

CLOSED ON SUNDAYS.   Proprietor - E. J. SMITH.

The Mount Pleasant Tea House, photographed in 1905, well patronised by cyclists and an early motorist. In 1986, the house, minus its chimneys, has a modern extension to the south but still bears an Edwardian date on its gable. Refreshments are served to motorists who may reflect that the bridge visible in Dean Lane (right of modern photograph) was built for the Croydon, Merstham & Godstone Railway in the first years of the nineteenth century.

Kenley

They say, at Kenley, a Miss is as good as a Mile. I think TWO'S better.

Until the building of the railway in 1856 Kenley, which was originally part of the Parish of Coulsdon, was a small hamlet, consisting of farms, cottages and the mansions of wealthy land-owners. During the reign of Queen Victoria more mansions were built in the area, together with cottages for the servants and labourers employed on the larger estates. Riddlesdown which overlooks the Kenley valley was then almost treeless. In the early 1900s it became a popular meeting place for the many visitors from London, who came to Gardner's Pleasure Resort.

In 1905 many of the buildings in Norfolk Terrace on the Godstone Road had still to be completed. The house to the right of the horse and cart is now the post office. Kenley Station can be seen in the background with the goods yard (which no longer exists) in front of the station master's house.

The shops in the 'High Street' or Godstone Road as we know it today, were built in the period 1890-1910, although some of them were private residences until after the first World War. Riddlesdown to the right of the picture still had open spaces close to the road, which today is completely covered by bushes and trees.

The modern view has not changed very much, apart from yellow lines and the parked cars! The Village Stores was previously Walton, Hassell & Port, and originally owned by Mr. A. Wickings, grocer.

This view of the station was taken about 1905, when the staff consisted of the station master, the head porter, the booking clerk plus two porters to handle passengers' luggage and operate the goods yard, which was then adjacent to the station master's house.

Times have changed and today Roy Bêlanger runs the station single handed!
The train seen here is the latest 455 stock that came into service in May 1986.

In 1903 Station Road was the home of Peter Prior, who ran the local slaughter house and Mr. Webb who built carriages for the local land-owners.

The cottages in the background appear virtually unchanged apart from the addition of porches and TV aerials! The garage premises now owned by Marn, were opened by Pudney & Sims in 1953.
Prior to that the site was used by the Chemical Pipe and Vessel Company.

Tea Gardens, Kenley.

In the early years of this century the Tea Gardens, known as Gardner's, was a popular venue for visitors from London, who came by train, tram, bicycle or horse-drawn carriage, to sample the 'Home Comforts & Amusements' of this pleasure resort.

Today the house at 23 Godstone Road is all that remains of the resort which spread over the land on which Famet Gardens, Famet Close and Famet Walk were built.

GARDNERS PLEASURE RESORT RIDDLESDOWN, SURREY

During the August Bank Holiday of 1904, Mr. & Mrs. Gardner and their team of local ladies catered for 4000 visitors. Many arrived by horse-brake and as the horses and vehicles were led away to stables on the premises, the families went up the steps to sample the amusements that included swings, hoop-la, coconut-shy, donkey rides, a zoo and a miniature railway!

Souvenir stalls sold ice cream, post cards and china ornaments which had their own Riddlesdown heraldic emblem. The coat of arms had blue flowers on a white ground, the other squares being yellow. The coronet is yellow, with red jewels.

51

Kenley. Commemoration Hall.

Sonnie's school when he; alright

The Commemoration Hall was built by Sir Joseph Lawrence to mark the Diamond Jubilee of Queen Victoria. It stands on the Godstone Road at the foot of St. James Road on the Purley-Kenley boundary. The hall was later extended and modified before becoming a secondary school - the Purley County School for Boys during the first World War. The school later moved to Placehouse Lane, Old Coulsdon, but the hall continued as Roke Secondary School.

In September 1976, the premises were taken over by the Shaftesbury Independent School for 5-18 year olds.

Outside the school, on the side of Godstone Road stands a horse-trough and drinking fountain, built in 1897, which probably goes unnoticed by the many passing motorists!

Kenley House, Kenley Common, Surrey

The house was built on the site of Kenley Farm in 1845 for George Drew, one of the directors of the Caterham Railway Company. It later became the home of the Young family, who lived there until 1912. After being empty for a few years it was turned into a nursing home from 1917 until 1923.

During the second World War when it was owned by J.B.Edwards, the Whyteleafe building and engineering contractors, it was used for the manufacture of parts for invasion barges.

In 1978 Micro Consultants bought the estate and have tastefully restored the house and gardens as an administrative headquarters for Quantel Ltd., part of the UEI Group.

The Bristol Bulldog coming into land at Kenley Aerodrome around 1930 is flying over the old Hayes Lane. The road was diverted around the aerodrome in 1939. The new road was closed in 1940 for the duration of the war and was not reopened until 26th June 1946.

The old Hayes Lane is still visible in this modern view with a Viking sailplane of No.615 Squadron Air Training Corps coming in to land. The Surrey Hills Gliding Club also use the aerodrome but it is no longer used for powered flight.

The original 'Rose & Crown' Inn is thought to have been built in 1723, when it would have been a welcome halt for coach passengers on the old Lewes Road over Riddlesdown. It survived the motor-car age until 1929. Its successor was hit by a flying bomb on the 3rd August 1944.

The third 'Rose & Crown' has recently been extensively modernised by the brewers Friary Meux and renamed 'Rose's'.
The new image designed for the younger set is perhaps more in keeping with the pace of today's traffic along the Godstone Road!

Purley

OUR LOCAL-EXPRESS
Purley

Today, the Gatwick Express thunders through Purley, while other quieter trains serve a new generation of commuters from Purley station.

Network South-East, unveiled on 11th June 1986, promises fast, punctual, uncrowded and clean trains, far removed from the pre-electric variety depicted above in 1908.

Purley, near Croydon.

The tram terminus at Purley in 1903, with Purley Fountain under construction in the background. For many Londoners, Purley tram terminus meant the start of a pleasant walk up Godstone Road to Riddlesdown and Gardner's Tea Rooms and Pleasure Grounds.

Kimberley Terrace still stands today, 83 years on, as a reminder of the Boer War shortly after which it was built.

The Railway Hotel in 1903.
Originally the Caterham Junction Hotel built by the Caterham Railway Company about 1856 - the now derelict Railway Hotel awaits re-development in 1986.

The Fountain, Purley.

Purley Memorial Fountain, known to generations of travellers since its unveiling in 1904 by the Duchess of Albany, has moved three times from its original site above.

The Fountain was first moved a short distance south to the corner of Godstone Road and Brighton Road. Many years later it was hidden inside the East Surrey Water Company grounds nearby.

The Fountain Purley.   English & Buckingham

In August 1983 the Fountain was restored to grace the gardens of Purley Library at Banstead Road - just in time, as by mid 1986 its previous site looks set for a major upheaval, with the East Surrey Water Company intending to consolidate most local operations at Kenley.

In Edwardian times the junction of Banstead Road and Brighton Road was a quiet but well developed area.

In 1986 traffic roars northward through this junction, deceptively peaceful in our picture until the lights change!

REEDHAM SCHOOL, PURLEY, SURREY

In an area which owes much to institutions like hospitals, schools and asylums for its early development and growth, the Asylum for Fatherless Children, re-established in Purley by Andrew Reed in 1858 was a notable example. Renamed Reedham Orphanage in 1904, then Reedham School in 1950; it closed in 1980. Modern homes now occupy the site in Reedham Drive.

The School Buildings.

Established as the Warehousemen, Clerks and Drapers Schools in 1866 and opened by Edward, Prince of Wales, the school now known as Thomas More remains little changed in its outward appearance. In common with other nearby institutions, ivy has been removed in the interests of lower building maintenance costs!

In 1907 The Lord Roberts Temperance Inn, General Stores and Post Office was established at William Webb's Model Village in Upper Woodcote, Purley.

The former pond adjacent was, no doubt, used by neighbour Charles Wakeling, blacksmith and goose-keeper who lived at No. 4 Woodcote Village. His descendants continue the business of general smiths in Coulsdon in the 1980s.

Sanderstead

The earliest known reference to Sanderstead is in a ninth century Saxon Charter. In the tenth century the land was given to the Abbey of Hyde, Winchester, and remained in its hands until the Dissolution when it became part of the Gresham Estate. The illustration above gives a glimpse of Sanderstead Court (1676) which was demolished in 1958. Another building also demolished was the Old Rectory (1680). Rectory Court now stands on the site.

Lower Sanderstead grew up around the railway line, opened in 1884. Building gradually expanded in the direction of the old village on top of the hill. This, however, remained rural and unchanged until the final break up of the estate and the sale of the land for building. Many houses were built from the late 1920s onward, and upper and lower Sanderstead were joined.

All Saints' Church (c. A.D. 1240) has a splendid site on the crest of the hill. With the growth of population after 1930 an enlargement plan was put in hand but not fully completed due to the advent of war. In 1981 a further enlargement was successfully accomplished.

The Addington Road was widened alongside the church in 1937. Road works carried out in 1971-72 destroyed "The Cutting" the name given to the last remaining stretch of the old lane which led down the hill towards Croydon. The roundabout by the pond also dates from this time.

Sanderstead Village Post Office

James Frosel started this shop in the early 1880s, and for close on fifty years it was the only shop in Sanderstead Village. There being no public house the shop had a licence, carried on by later owners, Smith and then Allison, to sell Beers, wines and spirits "to be consumed off the premises".

The 1930s brought competition from the new parade of shops across the road. Here the shop was extended into the left side of the cottage and the windows changed to plate glass. In 1985 the present owners of Cullens Stores made further alterations, but the cottage outline remains. In 1986 the assistant manageress is Jane Birch.

Mayfield Road, in lower Sanderstead, connects Sanderstead Road with Selsdon Road on the eastern side of the railway line which opened in 1884. Laid out on what must have been open hillside, many of the houses date from the 1890 to 1914 period, but a more modern one can be seen tucked in here and there. A short road to the left leads to the station.

Although the modern photograph depicts the road almost as peaceful as in the older scene, it is, in fact, a very busy thoroughfare made hazardous by many vehicles parked in the road, the older houses having no garage.

New houses created a need for local shops, and so Station Parade was built on the Sanderstead Road. The upper two blocks, commencing from the corner of Station Approach, are stepped to overcome the quite considerable slope. They present an unusual facade, with a pair of sash windows on the first floor and one large four pane window above.

The top shop underwent considerable rebuilding when it became Barclays Bank, though the outline remains similar. The fourth shop down, now Midland Bank, has been given a mock Georgian facade.

The Ladies of Mary made their third foundation in England when St. Anne's College was opened in September 1909 as a Boarding and Day School. It was situated on the corner where St. Mary's Road meets Sanderstead Road, and at the rear the grounds extended down to Purley Oaks Road.

For some years the original main building was adequate, but from 1930 on there was expansion. A separate building was erected for the Preparatory school, and a complete new wing added to the main block for the Senior School.

In the later 1970s a decision was made to close the school, and the last children departed at the end of the 1980 summer term. In October 1980 demolition started. It was not until 1983 that the present flats and houses began to rise on the site. This photograph shows the gates on the corner which remain to remind, or to puzzle, the passer by!

Warlingham

WARLINGHAM

PARISH TEA

IN THE BOARD SCHOOL
THURSDAY. JAN 2ND 1902
TEA AT 6.
ENTERTAINMENT AT 7
TICKETS TO BE HAD AT
VICARAGE,SCHOOL-HOUSE
OR THRO' DISTRICT VISITORS
PRICE - 6d BEFOREHAND
9d AT DOOR

Well into the early decades of this century Warlingham, with its remote hilltop position, remained an agricultural area. At the time of the 1866 enclosure two pieces of the common land were set aside for the use of the local people. The smaller piece, at the extreme western corner, already had a few buildings beside it, and this, now called The Green, is the centre of modern Warlingham.

All Saints' Church (c.A.D.1250) stands some way off in the direction of Crewes, now no longer a farm. The former Vicarage, now a private residence, and the Almshouses, both buildings dating from the 1670s, stand by the second open space. This was called The Common Recreation Ground, but today is usually called The Common. A motorbus service to Croydon started in 1921, and along with the motorcar probably brought about more change to the village than the influence of the railway.

Hamsey Green, Warlingham.

In 1866 Hamsey Green Pond was described as being one rood, fifteen perches (over 1600 square yards), by far the largest in Warlingham. The oldest of these photographs is 1910, when the main development of Hamsey Green was still twenty years ahead.

The second photograph is 1950, just before the post-war building phase started, and the third is 1986. The pond still remains, behind the railings on the right, but today is very small indeed when compared to its size in earlier years.

The Leather Bottle inn stands at the westernmost end of the old pre-enclosure common. The inn is listed as dating in part from the 18th century, and the old photograph shows the weatherboarded facade of the 1870s. It has since undergone several stages of rebuilding. The cottages on the right were demolished in 1906. The stone at the foot of the inn sign is probably a way-marker, and it is at this point that the route in the direction of the Caterham valley branches away from the main road.

Yew Tree Cottage, Warlingham.

This rural scene of cottages and thatched barns was photographed in 1903. In 1905 the barns were demolished, and Bradford Buildings erected on the corner site. The gateway on the extreme left of this scene is that of the first Wesleyan Chapel (1839).

Today the shell of Yew Tree Cottage still stands, and the chimneys can be seen rising above the modern extension. The site of the Chapel has been a garage since 1914.

Warlingham Village

From the corner of The Green the road divides, the main route going east towards the Weald, while the other leads towards Farleigh. This view of around 1910 shows the row of nine elms which stood outside The White Lion. The last was removed in 1978. The cottage on the left later became a shop.

In the recent view a modern addition rather overpowers the former cottages.

In the distance the eye is drawn to the splendid Turkey Oak, which used to be eclipsed by the elms. Devon House, on the right, dates from the late 1930s.

The White Lion, as with many older buildings, has grown and altered over the years. The earliest part is attributed to the 17th century. This photograph shows the inn before the rebuilding of the righthand wing, a modernization probably carried out in the 1890s. The Carrier's cart, going to and from Croydon, would have called here.

The righthand wing was given the neo-Tudor look in the 1930s. Over the door of the bar is the message 'Weary traveller, do ye mind your hatte', and just here at the door is the only place in the village centre where it is possible to see how much lower the road must have been in the past.

Croydon Mental Hospital, renamed Warlingham Park Hospital, was officially opened in 1903, and these houses were built at that time. Edward and Sydney Murrell started this shop in the Harrow Road, and for over eighty years it has remained the only shop in this Warlingham/Farleigh boundary area.

In 1976, despite much local protest, the Post Office counter facilities were withdrawn.

In 1891 Walter Blanchard purchased land, including two cottages, in Farleigh Road. The older photograph, of about 1905, shows him standing outside his forge. The Blanchard family were here until the early 1950s. Forge Cottage, now one dwelling, remains as a reminder of this past activity. The house is listed as dating from the 18th. century.

Today a modern house stands on the site of the forge. The road has been widened, and beyond, on the far left, is Paddock Cottage (1859).

The second Wesleyan Chapel was built in 1871, and enlarged in 1908. "Homeville" dated 1878, where Joel Ward, an Elder of the Chapel lived, stands beyond it, and, obscured by trees, is the butcher's shop. The Chapel site was restricted, so in 1960 a third Chapel was built, and this one demolished.

It is now over twenty five years since the site was sold. Considerable tree growth fills the corner and, regrettably, litter. "Homeville", later known as "Archdale", is now a restaurant.

Warlingham School.

The Board School was built in 1874, and opened with 75 pupils, some of whom came up from Whyteleafe. It was enlarged in 1885, and again in 1894. After the local Council was formed in 1896, the name was changed to the Council School. The Common Recreation Ground, on which the school stands, gradually became known as School Common. This view is about 1903.

Recent years have brought a decline in the number of children in the district. Eventually in July 1982, and not without local protest, this school was closed. It still stands empty in 1986, awaiting - who knows what?

Whyteleafe

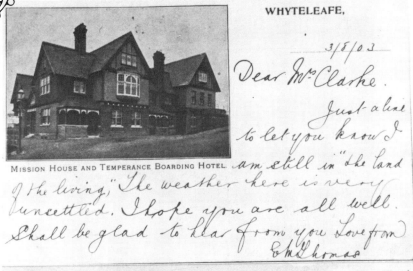

WHYTELEAFE,

3/8/03

Dear Mr Clarke.

Just a line to let you know I am still in "the land of the living." The weather here is very unsettled. I hope you are all well. Shall be glad to hear from you Love from

E M Thomas

MISSION HOUSE AND TEMPERANCE BOARDING HOTEL

The origins of the Gothic spelling of Whyteleafe are a little obscure, but appear to date from the mid-1800s. The development of the district began with the coming of the railway in 1856.

The photographs on this page show the Tabernacle, built for the Charity Commissioners in 1892. It passed to the Salvation Army in 1929, and was demolished in 1966 to make way for a car park.

Whyteleafe, looking south-west, from the Riddlesdown Quarry in 1904. The photograph shows the Bourne in flood. At that time there were two gas-holders, one belonging to the Kenley and Caterham Gas Company, the other to the Croydon Gas Company. Before they merged the Companies had premises on opposite sides of the main road.

Today only one gas-holder remains but the area has seen much development.

The parade of shops in Godstone Road, looking north, through the centre of Whyteleafe c.1915.

Apart from the shop fronts and the names of the owners little has changed in more than seventy years!

The name of the ironmonger H.W. Nott can still be seen on the wall of the first shop.

5826. Church Road, Whyteleafe.

Church Road, Whyteleafe, looking towards the Church from the level crossing, c. 1905. The barn which was pulled down in 1911, has made way for a block of flats.

The two flint covered houses in the centre of the old photograph, can still be seen through the trees.

A view of the level crossing from Whyteleafe Hill, c. 1910. Steam gave way to power in 1928.

Automatic level crossing gates control the many cars that now use Whyteleafe Hill, although few can be seen in this view!

The bridge carrying the Oxted Line at the bottom of Hillbury Road, c.1908. In the distance is the junction with the Godstone Road. The father, giving his child a ride on the bicycle, seems little concerned at the other traffic!

Double yellow lines, white lines and a modern lamp standard are some of the changes in today's view.

Godstone Road looking south, from Rose Cottage at the corner of Maple Road, towards "The Square" c.1915.

In these photographs, and those on the following pages, a surprising amount of old Whyteleafe remains.

Many houses may have a modern look, roads and pavements may have been made up, but in general, the present plan of the village along the Godstone Road is as it was in the early 1900s.

A view of the "Square" looking north towards Riddlesdown, c.1915.

Every building in this photograph remains today. But you dare not walk in the middle of the road now!

GODSTONE RD WHYTELEAFE 1185   W.T.C.

The corner of Hillbury Road, (originally Workhouse Lane), and the main Godstone Road c. 1908.

This corner of the village is due for redevelopment if a recent council plan to revitalise Whyteleafe comes into being.

The corner shop remained a newsagents and sweet shop until about two years ago, when it was converted into a private residence.

Post Office Square, Whyteleafe. 1

The first Whyteleafe Post Office can be seen in the centre of the shops on the right of the "old" photograph c. 1915.
It has since moved further up the main road on the left.

Woldingham

The descendants of Richard de Clare of Tonbridge, owned Woldingham until the 16th. century.

In the 13th. century a quarrel between the then owner, Gilbert de Clare, and the local administrator, Sir John Wauton, resulted in the manor being divided into two parts. The smaller part, Nether Court, took the land to the north of the village green, and the larger part of the division called Upper Court, took the land to the south.

Upper Court was retained by the de Clares as their family seat.

The story of Woldingham until the early 1800s is very much the story of the quarrels and bargainings of the various owners of Upper and Lower Court and the nearby Marden Estates.

As in so many other places, the development of the present day Woldingham began with the coming of the railways. The Oxted Line opened in 1884.

A view from about half-way up Station Hill around 1920. The open countryside is now obscured by trees and scrub.

Nether Court Farm around 1905. Both Nether and Upper Court Farms originally had their own ponds. The pond in front of Nether Court finally disappeared when Slines Oak Road was made up.

The same view today shows the edge of the car park belonging to the Roman Catholic Church, St. Edward the Confessor, that was built in 1971.

Woldingham Station in the early 1900s. When the station originally opened in 1884, it was called Marden Park. Access to and from Marden Park was made for the Greenwell family.

Apart from the parked cars and the white lines little has changed over the years.
A gate into the park from the up platform still exists today.

The Village Green, Woldingham.

Woldingham Supply Stores Series. 1004

A view of the Village Green c. 1910. The house on the corner of the Green used to be the Hop Pole Beer House in the middle 1800s. The Inn became popular with railway workers when they were building the line in the early 1880s but it was later closed by a local land-owner Mr. William Gilford.

The building later became the Tea Tree, a tea and guest house and today is the Village Stores.

The Bourne at the Viaduct. Caterham Valley

The Woldingham Railway Viaduct in the 1904 Bourne floods, taken from opposite Viaduct Lodge.

Today the side arches of the viaduct are almost completely overgrown with trees. Birchwood Lodge, the house on the left of the old photograph is now obscured from view.

Index

This provides an index to the main streets, buildings etc. in the Bourne Society area but does not include every establishment due to lack of space.